Mommy,
You have my ♡

forever and always.

creating your Book

You're going to love every step of creating your Binding Tales storybook! Here are a few pointers to help guide you in the right direction.

Tip #1
Start by reading through the entire book with an adult. This will help you think about how the story will unfold as you are writing and drawing pictures.

Tip #2
Use our free coloring sheets for practice sketching and coloring. Printed sheets are included with membership, or you can download them at bindingtales.com/freebies.

Tip #3
Ask questions (espcially if you get stuck) and work together. Working together as a team adds to the fun!

Tip #4
The paper in your book works best with pencils, crayons and colored pencils.

Tip #5
Be creative and have fun, there's no limit to your imagination.

Tip #6
Inspire others with your masterpiece! Take a picture while you show off your favorite pages of the finished book and tag @BindingTales on social media!

Co-authoring a book is something to be very proud of! **GREAT job!** *We're proud of you!*

This book was made with love.

For my Mommy

written and illustrated by:

_____

_____

year

With a little inspiration from Binding Tales.
Always make time to read, write and create ~ together.

My Mommy

My mommy is amazing because

_____

_____

_____

_____

I love when my mommy helps me

_____

_____

_____

_____

My favorite things to do with mommy are

_____

_____

_____

_____

_____

When we do things together it makes me feel

_____

_____

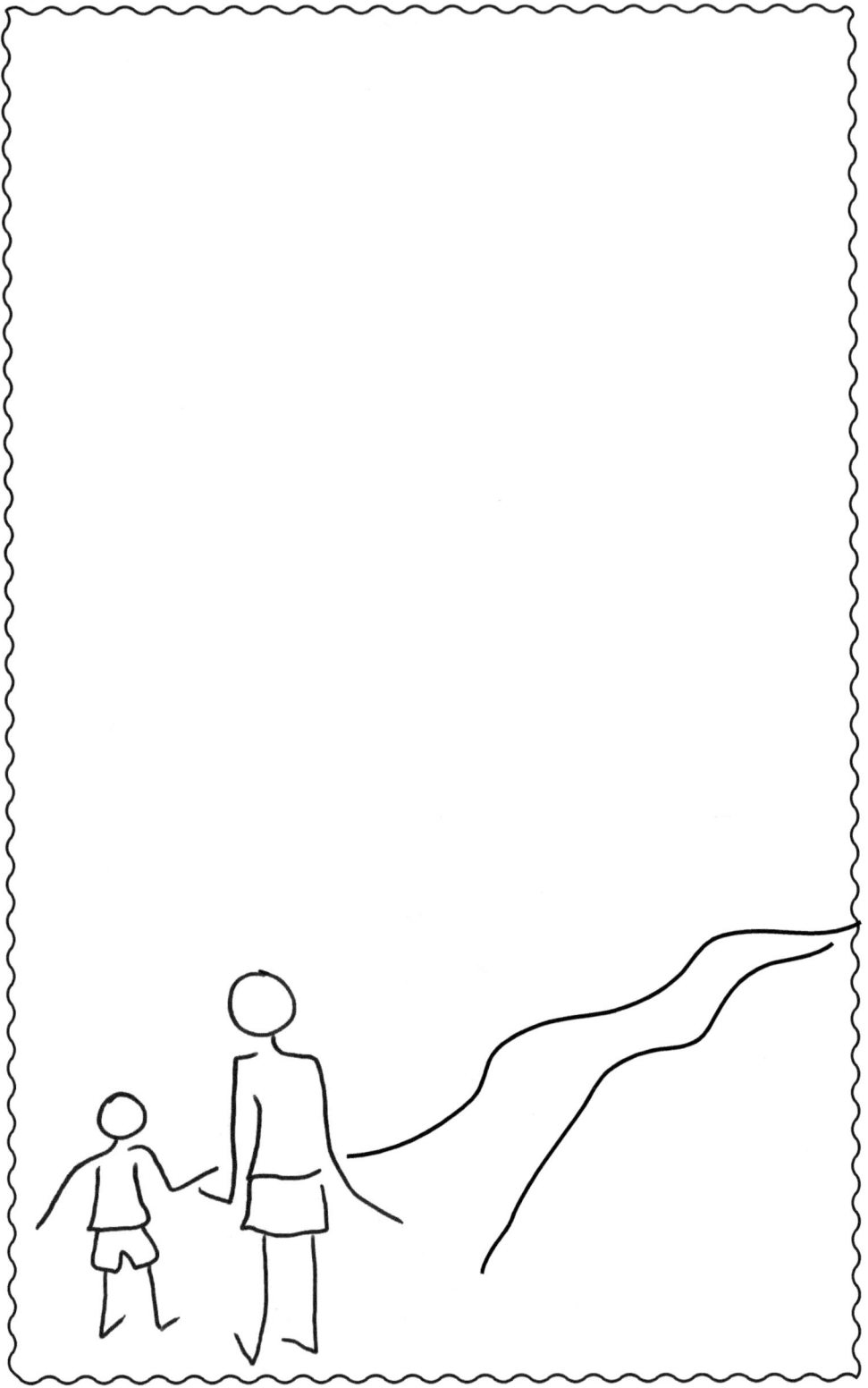

My favorite place to go with
my mommy is

_____

_____

_____

because we always

_____

_____

One time we even

_____

_____

_____

I believe that my mommy is a SUPERHERO because

_____

_____

_____

_____

Three of her super powers are

_____

_____

_____

_____

My favorite book to read with
mommy is

_____

_____

_____

My favorite part of the story is when

_____

_____

_____

_____

I know my mommy loves me because

_____

_____

_____

_____

_____

Something I love most about my mommy is

_____

_____

_____

_____

Mommy & Me

My mommy's favorite flower is

_____

_____

My mommy's favorite food is

_____

because
_____

_____

RELAX

Mommy really needs a break now and then.
My mommy likes to relax by

_____

_____

_____

My favorite way to help mommy is to

_____

_____

_____

when I look into the future, I will
be spending time with my mommy

_____

_____

_____

and we will

_____

_____

_____

_____

Binding Tales

Welcome to Binding Tales, bound paperback books that inspire and guide young authors with guided composition and illustration prompts to create their very own storybooks!

Your child's imagination has poured onto these pages, instantly preserving their priceless creation for you to cherish forever. *How cool is that?*

Our hope is that Binding Tales helps your family capture and create memories of your own. As our library of books grows, we would be honored to share in the growth of your young author!

Your Creativity Co-Contributors,

The Binding Tales Family

Hillary, Adam, Eva & Tyler Dow

Why stop with one? Once your young author catches the writer's itch they'll want to keep going! Binding Tales offers twelve and six-month memberships, with a growing library of themes.

memberships for young Authors

Your young author will receive a new book delivered right to their mailing address, with a new pencil & eraser, art supplies, a bookmark, sticker sheet, and practice coloring sheets to add to their writer's nook and artist's studio. As a critical team member, YOU will bask in the glorious convenience of being a rock star book contributor while not having to lift a finger every month for the books and activities to keep coming!

$18.95/month	$24.95/month
One Book Included	Two Books Included

Payment Options: Monthly, Semiannual, Annual
Single books sold on Amazon and BindingTales.com.

Be sure to like & follow our pages on social media!

JOIN TODAY
www.BindingTales.com

Thank you!

· FOR YOUR SUPPORT ·

REQUEST

Thank you for creating your very own Binding Tales book!

It would mean the world to me if you could take a short minute to leave a review on Amazon, as your kind feedback is much appreciated and so very important.

https://www.amazon.com/author/hillarydow

Thank you very much for your support and valuable time!

Hillary

Inspiring young authors to write and imagine.

First edition April 2019

www.BindingTales.com

www.ingramcontent.com/pod-product-compliance
Lightning Source LLC
Chambersburg PA
CBHW060608030426
42337CB00019B/3667